Birthday Suite

By Helen C. Pace

Illustrated by Roberta Wilson

© 2001 by Helen C. Pace
International Copyright Secured
ALL RIGHTS RESERVED
Unauthorized copying, arranging, adapting, or recording
is an infringement of copyright.
Infringers are liable under the law.

 Lee Roberts Music Publications, Inc.
Chatham, New York

DISTRIBUTED BY
 HAL•LEONARD
CORPORATION
7777 W. BLUEMOUND RD. P.O. BOX 13819 MILWAUKEE, WI 53212

The Invitations

Teacher

Happily

f

mf

Dear Ann and Mar-ty: I'm hav-ing a par-ty! Won't you come and play with me?

broaden

Par - ty time's from one 'til three. Dear Josh and Pol - ly: Do come to my par - ty!

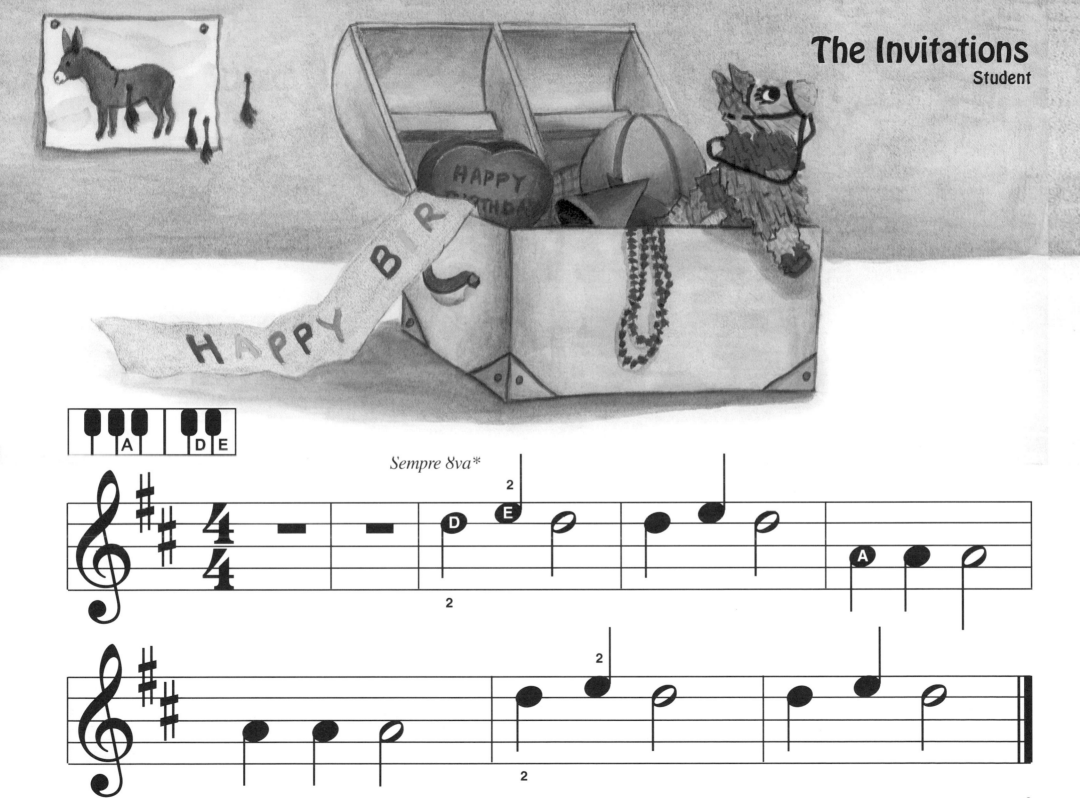

The Invitations
Student

Sempre 8va*

*Play 1 octave higher than written, throughout.

3

Birthday Hooray

Teacher

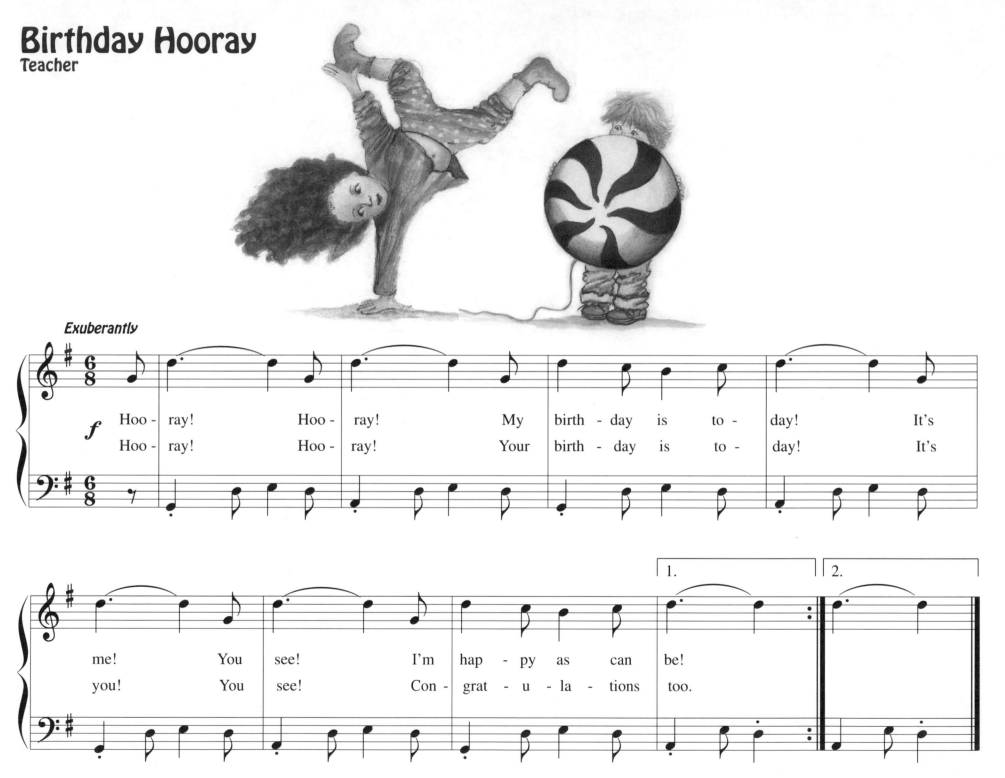

Exuberantly

f

Hoo - ray!   Hoo - ray!   My birth - day is to - day!   It's
Hoo - ray!   Hoo - ray!   Your birth - day is to - day!   It's

me!   You see!   I'm hap - py as can be!
you!   You see!   Con - grat - u - la - tions too.

1.

2.

4

Birthday Hooray
Student

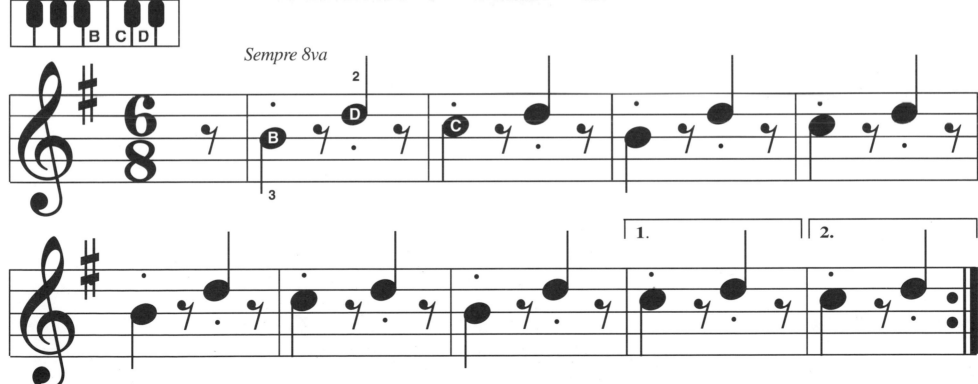

Baking the Cake

Teacher

With a gentle swing

mf Mix — ing the cake to be read — y by noon.
Pret — ty bright can - dles I'll take from the box.

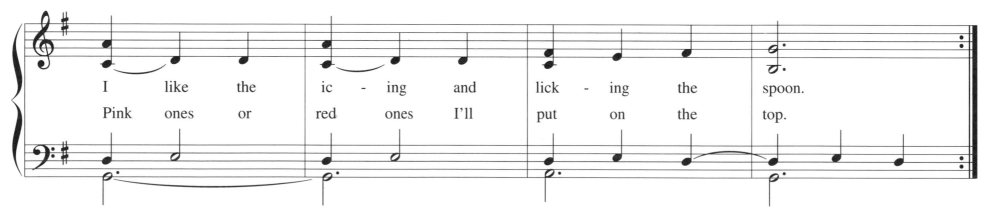

I like the ic - ing and lick - ing the spoon.
Pink ones or red ones I'll put on the top.

2383

Baking the Cake
Student

Doorbell Song

Teacher

Happily

Doorbell Song
Student

Happy Birthday

Teacher

Joyfully

Hap - py Birth - day! Hap - py Birth - day! Don't you
Birth - day! Hap - py Birth - day! Come and

love to have a par - ty on your Birth - day? Hap - py
o - pen up your pre - sents, It's your Birth - day!

1.
2.

Happy Birthday
Student

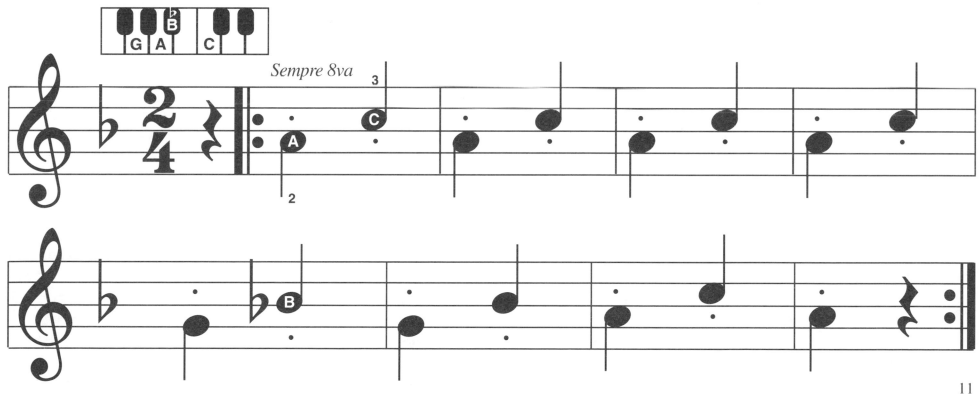

What A Surprise!
Student

Sempre 8ba*
*Play 1 octave lower than written, throughout.

2383

What A Surprise!
Teacher

Moderate Tempo

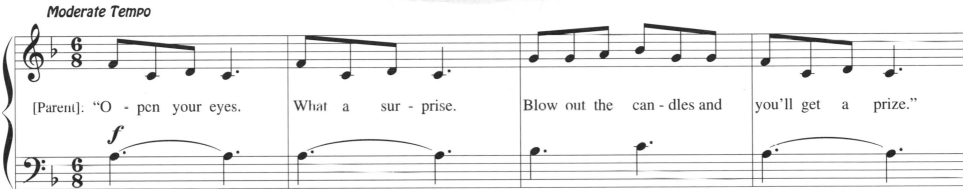

[Parent]: "O - pen your eyes. What a sur - prise. Blow out the can - dles and you'll get a prize."

[Child]: "What do I see? Look - ing at me! Wig - gly and fur - ry, It's soft as can be."

A Surprise Gift!

Teacher

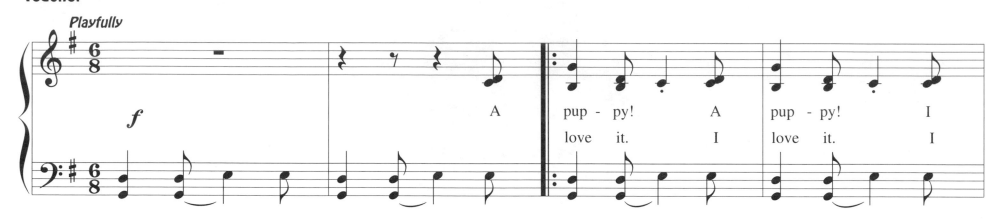

A pup - py! A pup - py! I
love it. I love it. I

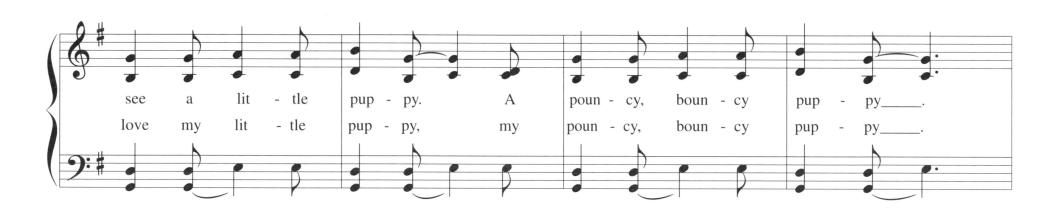

see a lit - tle pup - py. A poun - cy, boun - cy pup - py____.
love my lit - tle pup - py, my poun - cy, boun - cy pup - py____.

Is it just for me?! I Yo! Hap - py Birth - day!

A Surprise Gift!
Student

Sempre 8va

Another Surprise
Teacher

Gently

A kit - ty, a kit - ty, I see a pret - ty kit - ty. A
love it! I love it. I love my lit - tle kit - ty, that

fur - ry, pur - ry, kit - ty.
fur - ry, pur - ry, kit - ty.

ritard
1. Is it just for me? I

2. What a Hap - py Birth-day__!

Another Surprise
Student

What to Do?

Teacher

Moderato

f [Excitedly]: "Tell me what to do! Tell me what to say!

mf [Calmly]: "Qui - et is the best. She must have her rest.

May I pet her? Can't I pet her? Will she run a - way?"

Let her meet you, gent - ly greet you, when she feels it's best."

18

What to Do?
Student

Lullaby for Pets

Teacher

Gently

Cud - dly kit - ty, (pup - py)   soft and warm,   ly - ing gent - ly   in my arms,

While she's sleep - ing (he's)   we must be   quiet as mous - ies   e're could be.

ritard

20

Lullaby for Pets
Student

Sempre 8va

La Piñata
Teacher

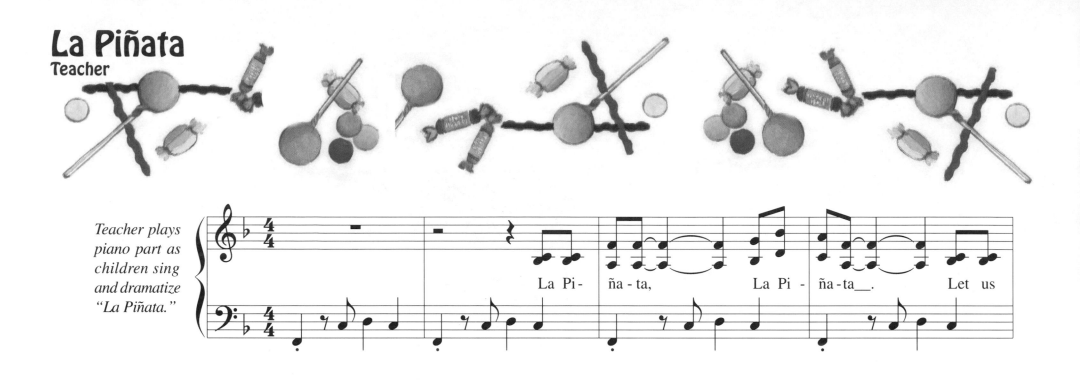

Teacher plays piano part as children sing and dramatize "La Piñata."

La Pi - ña - ta, La Pi - ña - ta__. Let us

see what we can find in the Pi - ña - ta__. La Pi - ña - ta__, La Pi - ña - ta__. Take a

Sing one octave lower than written

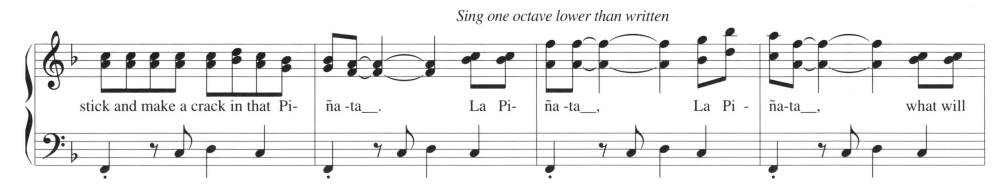

stick and make a crack in that Pi- ña -ta__. La Pi- ña -ta__, La Pi - ña-ta__, what will

22

spill up-on the floor from the Pi- ña -ta__? O some can-dy, Yes lots of can-dy__, will sure-ly

Sing as written

spill up-on the floor from the Pi- ña-ta__, and some rai-sins, Yes some rai-sins! La Pi -

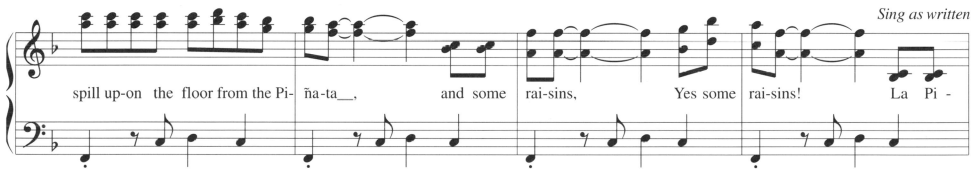

broaden   *a tempo*

ña - ta__, La Pi - ña - ta__. *ff* Hey! O - le!

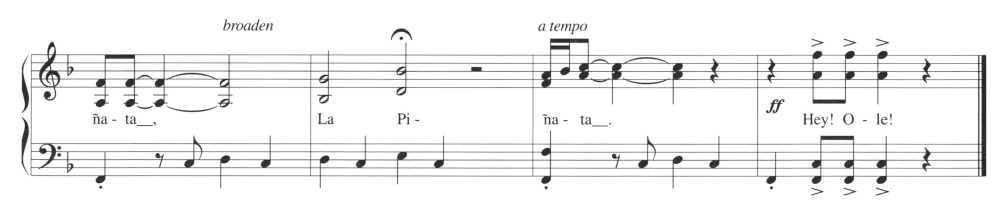

2383

23

Goodbye Song
Teacher

Moderato

mf Good - bye now, I thank you, what fun we had to - day. Good-

bye now. I'll see you. To - mor - row we will play.

Goodbye Song
Student

U.S. $7.95

ISBN 0-6340-3675-0

0 73999 87027   5

HL00372383